Slow Down Sister

*31 Days of
Giving God Control*

SLOW DOWN

Sister

31 DAYS OF
GIVING GOD CONTROL

Brittany Traylor

Ashland Ink

Published by Ashland Ink Publishing,
a division of Bell Asteri Publishing & Enterprises, LLC
209 West 2nd Street #177
Fort Worth TX 76102

www.ashlandink.com

Published in the United States of America

ISBN: 978-1-963514-15-5 (paperback)
ISBN: 978-1-963514-16-2 (hardback)

Introduction

In this fallen world, sometimes, it's all we can do to put one foot in front of the other. Trying to be a good daughter, wife, mother, employee, and friend can often feel daunting. We want to be intentional with Christ and each other, but something else always seems to take priority. When we can't seem to conquer everything and figure it all out on our own, we often end up feeling like failures. Though life feels overwhelming, Christ continually calls us toward Him. He wants us to confess our need and breathe in His peace. He is our helper and where we struggle most is trying to do enough and be enough. We can be so task-oriented and outcome-oriented that we miss the whole point of life here on Earth. He is there to walk beside us, to teach us, to love us, to guide us, and to direct us in his will. We are so busy being in control that we have forgotten that we aren't actually in control at all.

Throughout my life - motherhood, adoption, seasons of loss and illness, marital uncertainty, career changes, and big decisions for the kids - I've worried and fretted and planned and replanned. All to end up in a world filled with chaos, discontentment, and frustration. It wasn't until I surrendered in each of those areas that I began to have peace in each situation. One thing I have learned along the way is that I'm a control freak, addicted to trying to control so many aspects of my life. And I relapse a lot. Many times in life, I surrender and allow God to take complete control of my life. Then, a new season comes along, and I revert to taking matters into my own hands and relying on my own strength once more. Over time, though, I'm learning to loosen that grip of illusioned control more and more. Plans are good, but they can't be our god.

As a high school teacher, students come to me often, stressing about their future plans. I find myself telling them things like, it's okay, you don't have to have it all figured out at 17. But honestly, sis, each time I say it, God reminds me that that statement rings true through all of our years. We don't have to have it figured out at 27, or 37, or even 87. We are called to walk in his love and trust him ALL THE DAYS OF OUR LIVES. In all seasons of life and all aspects of life. Plans are good, but they can change in the blink of an eye. That's why our happiness can't be found in the expectation of our future or in the figuring out of our tomorrows. Instead, we have to learn to worship in the wind and the wilderness, in the calm and in the chaos, and in the certainties and the uncertainties of this wild ride called life.

We don't have to keep holding on, figuring out, and controlling every little aspect of our lives; we are simply called to surrender and do the following. It's not until we let go and stop trying to figure it out in our own strength that God can work the way he sees fit. *Sis, you don't have to have it all figured out.* There is beauty in giving something over to an all-knowing God and falling into the loving arms of our savior. I hope that this devotional serves as a reminder to future me and to you that we don't have to hold on so tight. We are called to LET GO and LET GOD WORK IT OUT ON OUR BEHALF AND FOR THE GLORY OF HIS KINGDOM.

I want to be in 100 places
And I am about to fall apart
Meet me here dear Jesus
Hold the worry in my heart

You hold yesterday and tomorrow
Every single day of the year
I know this truth in my head
That you would now let my heart hear

"Your power is made perfect through weakness"
When I'm at the end of me
Give me courage to let you lead, Lord
When I'm drowning in this sea

One breath at a time
Teach me to breathe your peace in
Finding victory over my thoughts
I will NOT let Satan win

Day One

CONTENT IN THE CHAOS

Scripture

"I am not saying this because I am in need, for I have learned to be content whatever the circumstances. I know what it is to be in need, and I know what it is to have plenty. I have learned the secret of being content in any and every situation, whether well fed or hungry, whether living in plenty or in want. I can do all this through him who gives me strength."
Philippians 4:11-13

I will give thanks to you, Lord, with all my heart; I will tell of all your wonderful deeds."
Psalm 9:1

Reflection

In my household of six, we have a mix of personalities, from loud to quiet, emotional to reserved. Our differences make life interesting, but it's rare for everyone to be happy at once. When one person thrives, others struggle. I see this in my own life, too. When my marriage is great, work falls apart. When I succeed at motherhood, I feel inadequate elsewhere. Yet, I'm reminded that we aren't called to perfection but to find contentment in our circumstances. Even in chaos, Scripture guides us toward His greater will. By letting go of the happiness checklist and embracing Jesus' practices, we can find peace even in the mess. If Paul can, Sis, so can you.

1. *Do you find it hard to be content when things aren't just so?*
2. *How do you think that Paul and the followers of Jesus found contentment in their situations?*

Guided Prayer

Dear God, you know I want things just so. I want to make the right decisions and make my family happy. You know I desire that every area of my life flow smoothly and stress-free. Since that isn't always the case, help me lean into your will instead. Help me be joyful, even when this world tries to steal my joy. Help me to be thankful no matter what my days bring, and help me to remain in constant communication with you so I can face each situation that comes my way in your strength. Lord, bring me to a place of contentment, even amid the chaos that so often surrounds me.

Personal Prayers

_____

_____

_____

_____

_____

_____

_____

_____

_____

_____

_____

_____

_____

_____

_____

_____

_____

_____

_____

_____

_____

_____

_____

_____ DATE

Day Two

PRUNING IN THE PAIN

Scripture

"He cuts off every branch in me that bears no fruit, while every branch that does bear fruit he prunes so that it will be even more fruitful. You are already clean because of the word I have spoken to you. Remain in me, as I also remain in you. No branch can bear fruit by itself; it must remain in the vine. Neither can you bear fruit unless you remain in me. "I am the vine; you are the branches. If you remain in me and I in you, you will bear much fruit; apart from me you can do nothing."
John 15:2-5

Reflection

I am no stranger to pain. Most of us are well acquainted with it. Reflecting on my most painful seasons, I can't honestly say, "I'm glad that happened." However, I can recognize how I've grown in the Lord during those times. This growth is particularly evident during moments of loss - both the loss of my mom and the loss of my sense of self. In both of those seasons, I found more of Jesus. He was there for me, even when I struggled to seek Him, and through these challenging experiences, He pruned me. He opened my heart, revealing how to grow in the spiritual realm. Instead of becoming bitter, I developed a deeper understanding. When we stay connected to the vine, we access a strength beyond our own. We learn to move in sync with the Spirit rather than being overwhelmed by our circumstances. Pain is a certainty in life, and if you're experiencing a painful season, I see you. But remember, Sis, there is pruning in the pain.

1. *Do you truly grasp the concept of pruning?*
2. *In what ways do you sense that God is pruning you now or has done so in the past?*

Guided Prayer

Dear Lord, Hold me close to you as I abide in your love. Be my vine and prune me as you see fit, even when the cutting back hurts. Hold me, Lord Jesus, and open my eyes to the areas in which I'm not being fruitful. Help me to grow in my ability to produce fruit and help me to follow hard after you in all areas. I love you, I trust you, and I want you to use me. Thy kingdom come.

Personal Prayers

_____

_____

_____

_____

_____

_____

_____

_____

_____

_____

_____

_____

_____

_____

_____

_____

_____

_____

_____

_____

_____

_____ DATE

Day Three

HOLINESS IS THE HURTING

Scripture

"Consider it pure joy, my brothers and sisters, whenever you face trials of many kinds, because you know that the testing of your faith produces perseverance."
James 1:2-3

Reflection

When I look back on the most hurtful times of my life, I can see how the Lord drew near to me. So often, we seek and try to get closer to God, but when stuff gets hard, we lose hope and hang our heads. But I'm learning that holiness happens in the hurting. Bethany Joy Scott said, "What is grace worth if I'm not willing to show up in my full authentic mess and let God guide me, heal me, grow me in that place?" This has been so very true in my life. It's in the hurting that we can be our most vulnerable with God and let him pull us unto himself. It's in the hurting that we can let go and be separate from ourselves, and that separation from our wills and this world is what pulls us toward holiness. That's why James tells us to count it joy during these times of hurt. It's in those times that we recognize what grace is. Sis, it's in the hurting you can find holiness.

1. *Do you believe God teaches us to be holy in our hurting?*
2. *What do you think it means to bring your full authentic mess to God?*

Guided Prayer

Lord, thank you for the trials, because what I want more than anything is to be holy. I pray for all of my friends and family who are in uncertain or hurtful seasons right now. May they experience grace like never before. When I start to think, why me? Why my family, remind me that I'm not in this boat alone. I hear you whisper, why not- I'm with you. Remind me that you still walk on water, calm storms, and comfort the weary. Thank you for all you are doing, all you have done, and all that you will do. I am wholly yours.

Personal Prayers

_____

_____

_____

_____

_____

_____

_____

_____

_____

_____

_____

_____

_____

_____

_____

_____

_____

_____

_____

_____

_____

_____

_____ DATE

Day Four

FEAR ISN'T FOR THE FREE

Scripture

"Since the children have flesh and blood, he too shared in their humanity so that by his death he might break the power of him who holds the power of death—that is, the devil—And free those who all their lives were held in slavery by their fear of death."
Hebrews 2:14-15

"But whoever looks intently into the perfect law that gives freedom, and continues in it—not forgetting what they have heard, but doing it—they will be blessed in what they do."
James 1:25

Reflection

Throughout my life I have faced many fears, and while I still experience fear at times, God has freed me of many crippling anxieties. When fear creeps up again, I'm reminded that fear isn't for those free in Christ. Jesus came to take away the greatest of all fears: a future of nothingness and lifelong separation from Him. His desire is that we live freely and love abundantly, trusting in him to alleviate our fear. James describes the law as the law of liberty, emphasizing that true freedom comes from following the law of love. Trade your fear for freedom, Sis, it's one of the many reasons why Jesus came.

1. *What fears are you having a hard time releasing to the Lord?*
2. *What fears has He given you peace from over the years?*

Guided Prayer

God, you know all my fears, both the silly and the serious. You know that Satan can come in and take the freedom you give and replace it with lies and fear in the blink of an eye. Help me to flee from fear as I learn to put my trust in you. Help me to realize that any fear that may come to pass is not born of your spirit. You still hold me, and being held by you is one of the greatest gifts. I release my fears and grab hold of your freedom today. Keep me in this space and bind the lies of Satan. Amen

Personal Prayers

_____

_____

_____

_____

_____

_____

_____

_____

_____

_____

_____

_____

_____

_____

_____

_____

_____

_____

_____

_____

_____

_____

_____

_____ DATE

Day Five

GUILT IS GONE

Scripture

"But for that very reason I was shown mercy so that in me, the worst of sinners, Christ Jesus might display his immense patience as an example for those who would believe in him and receive eternal life."
Timothy 1:16

Reflection

Far too often, I find myself looking over my day, my week, or my month with disappointment. I have so much guilt about how I could have been a better mom, sister, wife, or friend. In Paul's letter to his apprentice in the faith, Timothy, he addresses these feelings of inadequacy. Feelings of inadequacy will come because we can never be holy enough in our own strength. But, thankfully, Jesus closes that gap with mercy. The more we begin to grasp that, the less guilt we begin to have. He's a good, good God. Patient when we aren't all that we are called to be. In the gospels, Jesus didn't throw up his hands with his disciples when they got it wrong, He just continued to seek the Father, live by example, and spur them on in their faith through unconditional love. And Sis, he's still doing that for us today.

1. *Is there anything you've felt guilty about this week?*
2. *Is it a convicting type of guilt from the holy spirit, or is it a shaming guilt from the enemy?*

Guided Prayer

Lord, replace my feelings of guilt with an increased desire to please you. Lead me in the works you would have me do to further your kingdom, but remind me daily that it's not what I can and will do but what you have enabled and empowered me to do through your love and grace. Help me see the power and the beauty surrounding me rather than the sin and shame. Thank you for your perfect patience. I'm so undeserving but also so very thankful.

Personal Prayers

_____

_____

_____

_____

_____

_____

_____

_____

_____

_____

_____

_____

_____

_____

_____

_____

_____

_____

_____

_____

_____

_____

_____

_____

_____ DATE

Day Six

WORSHIP IN THE WILDERNESS

Scripture

"So, as the Holy Spirit says: 'Today, if you hear his voice,
do not harden your hearts as you did in the rebellion, during the time of
testing in the wilderness, where your ancestors tested and tried me,
though for forty years they saw what I did.'"
Hebrews 3:7-9

Reflection

Moses, being led by the Lord, led the Israelites out of slavery and toward
freedom. However, this journey took place largely in the wilderness.
When I think of wilderness, I think of emptiness, feelings of being alone,
and just a generally long journey. I've had many wilderness-like seasons in
my life. Seasons where I wondered what God was doing and why he led
me there. I worried and planned, had days filled with fear and frustration,
and did my fair share of complaining. Instead of drowning out his voice
with our moaning and groaning, it's in the wilderness we are called to
trust. It's in the wilderness that we are called to recognize his works and,
above all, to worship. It is only in our worship that he can prove his
power, and it is in our worship that we are reminded that walking with
Him will always be worthwhile. Keep trucking through the wilderness,
Sis, He's still worthy of worship.

1. *What seasons of wilderness have you endured?*
2. *Did you find it difficult to worship?*

Guided Prayer

God, I can't always see the blessings in the wilderness. It's so hard for me to trust and worship in these times, but I know your plans are for good, and my future and the future of my family are secure in your hands. Help me, dear Jesus, to worship you for all you are and all you will do! Help me not to harden my heart in the trials and worship, no matter how long it takes for me to see the promise.

Personal Prayers

_____
_____
_____
_____
_____
_____
_____
_____
_____
_____
_____
_____
_____
_____
_____
_____
_____
_____
_____
_____
_____
_____

_____ DATE

Day Seven

LORD LEAD ME
ONE DAY AT A TIME

Scripture

"Why, you do not even know what will happen tomorrow. What is your life? You are a mist that appears for a little while and then vanishes. Instead, you ought to say, 'If it is the Lord's will, we will live and do this or that.'"
James 4:14-15

Reflection

As a mom, you are required to plan to some degree. If we don't plan, things are left undone. Appointments must be made, gifts must be purchased, bills must be paid, and dinner must be cooked. In my life, I've found it difficult to let go of the need to plan everything out. I haven't fully stopped planning, but I'm learning, instead, to lean into the fact that provision is greater than planning. We can look forward without worrying because God has already planned how He will meet our needs. He's already taken care of tomorrow. He only asks that we take it one day at a time. So, in the planning, we just mustn't forget where our help comes from. In the preparation, we have to be ever aware of the provision of our provider. And when it all seems to go awry, we have to remember his promise above all. Plans are good, Sis, but our heart's cry should be, "Lead me, Lord, one day at a time!"

1. *Do you have a hard time letting go of your plans and allowing God to meet your needs?*
2. *In what area can you loosen your grip and take it one day at a time?*

Guided Prayer

Thank you, God, for giving me the ability and mental capacity to plan, but help me remember that your plans are above all. Help me to surrender daily as I only worry about today. Hold my tomorrows and remind me of your provision. Give me wisdom in the areas that I do need to preplan and help me to see your will in each area.

Personal Prayers

_____

_____

_____

_____

_____

_____

_____

_____

_____

_____

_____

_____

_____

_____

_____

_____

_____

_____

_____

_____

_____

_____

_____

_____

_____ DATE

Day Eight

HE'S THE KING OF THE WORLD

Scripture

"Jesus said, 'My kingdom is not of this world. If it were, my servants would fight to prevent my arrest by the Jewish leaders. But now my kingdom is from another place.' 'You are a king, then!' said Pilate. Jesus answered, 'You say that I am a king. In fact, the reason I was born and came into the world is to testify to the truth. Everyone on the side of truth listens to me.'"
John 18:36-37

Reflection

I'll never forget a particularly tough week I had several years back. I was doing hospice, and in a span of two days, I walked a 42-year-old mom of two through her last days of life, placed a 7-month-old hospice patient in the back of a hearse, and said goodbye to a lifelong friend with cystic fibrosis. I wasn't angry with God as much as I was just taken aback by the unfair nature of this world. I wrestled and struggled and fought to understand why. The answer was found in the lyrics of a Natalie Grant song. I had placed God within the walls of my mind, forgetting that He's King. I had to be reminded that this life is not all there is. It's a blessing that we get to live and coexist with one another, but at the end of the day, this is not our home. This world is not our forever, and death is not the end. Whatever you are going through, Sis, be reminded that we don't have to understand in order to trust. We may not be able to comprehend it all, but we can always be held by the King of the world.

1. Are there areas that you feel God's way is not good right now?
2. Even in those times of defeat, can you acknowledge that He is the king of the world?

Guided Prayer

Jesus, help me remember you are the king of the world. Help me trust you in ALL THINGS. Help me to remember that your ways are not our ways. When we see the messy knots and frays on the back of the tapestry, you see the beauty from your view. Thank you for being in control so I don't have to be. Help me to understand that it is in love you allow things and it is in faith we will be restored unto you someday.

Personal Prayers

_____
_____
_____
_____
_____
_____
_____
_____
_____
_____
_____
_____
_____
_____
_____
_____
_____
_____
_____
_____
_____
_____
_____
_____

_____ DATE

Day Nine

CALLED TO BE COUNTERCULTURAL

Scripture

"You adulterous people, don't you know that friendship with the world means enmity against God? Therefore, anyone who chooses to be a friend of the world becomes an enemy of God. Or do you think Scripture says without reason that he jealously longs for the spirit he has caused to dwell in us?"James 4: 4-5

Reflection

Raising children in today's society has made me increasingly aware of how easily we can be influenced by our culture. Last year, socks from the '80s were considered out of style, yet they are now back in style. Every day, new and quirky words enter our vocabulary and gain acceptance. Just last week, my 7-year-old remarked, "Ma, I'd rather be a liar than a loser," while trying to impress his friends. Adults experience similar pressures, striving for influencer-worthy holidays, jobs, and lifestyles. However, through James, God reminded us 2,000 years ago that this pursuit does not lead to true happiness. He doesn't object to our desire for nice things, goals, or style; rather, it becomes problematic when our longing for these things comes between our hearts and His. He desires our devotion, and His immense love makes Him unable to bear seeing us invest our time and energy in the fleeting trends of our culture. Dare to be counter-cultural, Sis.

1. *What parts of the world are you holding on to tighter than you are holding on to the robe of Jesus?*
2. *Are you stewarding yourself in this life to be a friend of the world or a friend of your Father in heaven?*

Guided Prayer

Sweet Jesus, help me let go of all that the world says I should have and do. Help me to seek first the kingdom, and then all the things will be given to me...things of your will, not this fleeting world. Help me to stand against all that is not of you. Help me to hold fast to your truth. Help me to see through your lens of love and not judge. Help me to remove the idols and seek you first as I seek to become a countercultural Christian. Thank you for longing for me like you do.

Personal Prayers

_____

_____

_____

_____

_____

_____

_____

_____

_____

_____

_____

_____

_____

_____

_____

_____

_____

_____

_____

_____

_____ DATE

Day Ten

GOD IS GREAT AND HE WILL MAKE IT GOOD

Scripture

"Taste and see that the Lord is good; blessed is the one who takes refuge in him."
Psalm 34:8

"God saw all that he had made, and it was very good. And there was evening, and there was morning—the sixth day."
Genesis 1:31

Reflection

In the beginning, there was God, and with him, there was nothingness. He spoke, and just like that, life happened. Plant life, animal life, and humanity were born. Creativity gave birth to diversity, and there were vast differences in all that he made. Fruits and vegetables. Day and night. Land and sea. Flying creatures and crawling ones. Man and woman. And he said it was GOOD. One of the things that made it so good was the beautiful distinctness of each part of His creation. God is great, and all that he makes is so, so good, even when it doesn't feel good or look good to you by earthly standards. In your need to figure it all out, be reminded, Sis, if it isn't looking so good now, or if it's different from what you thought it would be, He will make it all good in time because He is great. That has been true from the start of creation.

1. *Is there a situation that you aren't feeling good about at this time in your life?*
2. *Do you believe that he is still good in the midst? Or do you believe he can bring good from this situation?*

Guided Prayer

God, help me remember that when it doesn't feel good,
you are still great. Remind me of your goodness when I
only see and feel let down. Gratefulness closes our eyes to
all that we feel we don't have and opens our eyes to all that
we do. Help me live in a spirit of thankfulness for all that
you are and all that you do. Help me embrace all that is and
what will be, knowing your greatness holds me and my
future securely.

Personal Prayers

_____
_____
_____
_____
_____
_____
_____
_____
_____
_____
_____
_____
_____
_____
_____
_____
_____
_____
_____
_____
_____
_____
_____
_____

_____ DATE

Day Eleven

FIRM FOUNDATION

Scripture

"Therefore everyone who hears these words of mine and puts them into practice is like a wise man who built his house on the rock. The rain came down, the streams rose, and the winds blew and beat against that house; yet it did not fall, because it had its foundation on the rock."
Matthew 7:24-25

"For no one can lay any foundation other than the one already laid, which is Jesus Christ."
1 Corinthians 3:11

Reflection

Jesus was such a good teacher, and He did all the things great teachers do. He spoke with authority, he led by example, and he used examples that were practical and applicable to his audience. That audience was largely comprised of fishermen and builders. While I'm not a builder, I know that without a foundation, a building crumbles and falls apart. We have to have a foundation to stand. Jesus must be our foundation, the building block from which we shape and construct our lives. Without a cornerstone, things crumble, and chaos ensues. Without a firm foundation in Christ, there can be no purpose in our work, and we have nothing to lean on when it all gets heavy. Jesus wants to be the starting point and center of our lives, Sis.

1. *Is Jesus the Cornerstone of your life, your plans, and your decisions?*
2. *Do you feel he holds you steady in stormy times and uncertain seasons?*

Guided Prayer

Lord, let me learn to make you my foundation more each day. Thank you for being the cornerstone of my life. When all around me is crumbling and I don't know where to start, teach me to place you back at the top of my priorities and the center of my life. Scripture teaches with you as the building block, we will not crumble and fall. Help me stand secure in that promise today.

Personal Prayers

_____

_____

_____

_____

_____

_____

_____

_____

_____

_____

_____

_____

_____

_____

_____

_____

_____

_____

_____

_____

_____

_____

_____ DATE

Day Twelve

SEEK FIRST HIS KINGDOM

Scripture

"But seek first his kingdom and his righteousness, and all these things will be given to you as well."
Matthew 6:33

"The lions may grow weak and hungry, but those who seek the Lord lack no good thing."
Psalm 34:10

"You will seek me and find me when you seek me with all your heart."
Jeremiah 29:13

Reflection

As an adult who struggles with attention, one of my biggest difficulties is getting started. I look around and get overwhelmed by the task no matter how big or small - hang my head, procrastinate, and stress. Jesus, in his compassion, told us how to begin EVERY SINGLE TASK we will ever encounter. He said to seek first the kingdom of God, and he will take care of the rest. ADHD or not, we can all use some instruction on where to start from time to time. Seeking the Lord first in the big and small things of this life gives Him the glory He deserves, and it makes things so much more manageable for you, Sis.

1. *Are you seeking the Lord first in your decisions, relationships, and daily tasks?*
2. *Or do you find that you are trying to do things your way and then seeking him as an afterthought?*

Guided Prayer

Lord, thank you for planning it all out even before I was born, and thank you for giving me the tools and knowledge to know and seek you more. Help me be submissive in my search for you. Show me your ways and make my heart pliable before you. In my mothering, my occupation, and my future, help me seek you first. When I'm sad and when I'm stressed, remind me that you hold the answers, and my only job is to seek and surrender to your will in each situation and season.

Personal Prayers

_____
_____
_____
_____
_____
_____
_____
_____
_____
_____
_____
_____
_____
_____
_____
_____
_____
_____
_____
_____
_____
_____
_____
_____

_____ DATE

Day Thirteen

A HUMBLE HEART

Scripture

"He has shown you, O mortal, what is good. And what does the Lord require of you? To act justly and to love mercy and to walk humbly with your God."
Micah 6:8

"I tell you that this man, rather than the other, went home justified before God. For all those who exalt themselves will be humbled, and those who humble themselves will be exalted."
Luke 18:14

Reflection

Being a Boss Babe and a go-getter is admirable, but sometimes we need help. In our drive to succeed, we can forget our source and let pride creep in, pushing God aside as if to say, "I've got this." That mindset can be dangerous. God has been teaching me, through examples like Moses, David, and Jesus, that true strength comes from humility. Moses doubted his worthiness, but that's why he was chosen. David knew his strength was in the Lord, and Jesus exemplified ultimate humility. When we stay humble and rely on God's strength, we can accomplish everything He sets before us. Lay aside your pride, Sis, and He will be exalted.

1. *Are you a "I can do it all type person"?*
2. *Do you feel that this sometimes interferes with your ability and desire to lean on the Lord and others around you for help?*

Guided Prayer

God, I know you want to give us good things, both tangible and spiritual blessings. Help us first humble ourselves to you. Release us from all pride and feelings of self-preservation, and in humility, let us place our lives in your hands. You be the potter, teach us to be the clay. Mold us. Mend us and mature us in Christ's name. Amen.

Personal Prayers

_____

_____

_____

_____

_____

_____

_____

_____

_____

_____

_____

_____

_____

_____

_____

_____

_____

_____

_____

_____

_____

_____

_____ DATE

Day Fourteen

WISDOM FOR THE WEARY

Scripture

"If any of you lacks wisdom, let him ask of God, who gives to all liberally and without reproach, and it will be given to him."
James 1:5

"The fear of the Lord is the beginning of wisdom, and knowledge of the Holy One is understanding."
Proverbs 9:10

Reflection

Solomon had the opportunity to ask for anything in the Bible, and he chose wisdom; he asked God for the ability to apply knowledge and experience in making sound decisions and judgments. This quest for wisdom serves as the foundation for the title of this entire book. Nothing has inspired me to seek wisdom more than the journey of raising a family in today's world. I want to do everything right and get answers at the snap of my fingers so badly. In the opening of his proverbs, Solomon conveyed that the fear of the Lord is the beginning of wisdom. This fear is not the kind we typically think of; instead, it refers to a sense of reverence and complete awe of an all-knowing and all-powerful Father. To truly understand the ways of the Lord, we must first recognize and respect the omnipotence of the God we serve, Sis.

1. *Do you ever sit back in awe and wonder of all that God is and has done for you?*
2. *Do you find yourself searching for wisdom without first being reverent to the Lord?*

Guided Prayer

God, I know you want to give us good things, both tangible blessings and spiritual blessings. Help me to first humble myself to you. Release me from all pride and feelings of self-preservation. In humility, I place my life and the life of my family in your hands. Be the potter and teach me to be the clay. Mold me, mend me, and mature me in Christ. In Jesus' name. Amen

Personal Prayers

_____

_____

_____

_____

_____

_____

_____

_____

_____

_____

_____

_____

_____

_____

_____

_____

_____

_____

_____

_____

_____

_____

_____

_____

_____ DATE

Day Fifteen

ABIDE, ABIDE, ABIDE

Scripture

"And now, dear children, continue in him, so that when he appears we may be confident and unashamed before him at his coming."
1 John 2:28

"If you remain in me and my words remain in you, ask whatever you wish, and it will be done for you."
John 15:7

Reflection

My relationship with Christ often feels like taking one step forward and two steps back. While I experience growth in love, I struggle with self-control. I may be faithful in my relationships but find myself lacking joy. Jesus repeatedly urges his disciples to "ABIDE in me," inviting them to sit with him, endure alongside him, and remain anchored in his presence, even as he prepares to depart. We receive that same commandment and invitation today. He desires for us to abide in Him, Sis, staying steadfast in his love, regardless of the challenges we face. Only then can we navigate everything this world has to offer and be confident and ready for His return.

1. *What does abiding in Christ look like to you?*
2. *Do you sometimes see it as a chore to sit with Jesus, spend time in his word, or stand firm in your faith?*

Guided Prayer

Jesus, thank you for showing us what it looks like to abide in God. You were the greatest example of endurance and fruit of the Spirit because you drew away to meet with the Father and walked in his love continuously. Help me to be more like that! Help me to spend more time in the Word so that I can remain in your truth throughout the day. I look forward to the day that I abide in your love forever and the trials of this world are no more.

Personal Prayers

_____

_____

_____

_____

_____

_____

_____

_____

_____

_____

_____

_____

_____

_____

_____

_____

_____

_____

_____

_____

_____

_____

_____ DATE

Day Sixteen

A GLORIOUS GIFT-GIVER

Scripture

"Command those who are rich in this present world not to be arrogant nor to put their hope in wealth, which is so uncertain, but to put their hope in God, who richly provides us with everything for our enjoyment."
1 Timothy 6:17

"If you, then, though you are evil, know how to give good gifts to your children, how much more will your Father in heaven give good gifts to those who ask him!"
Matthew 7:11

Reflection

One of the most cherished roles I have in this life is that of a mother to four beautiful children. It is one of my greatest desires to love them well and bring them happiness. Jesus teaches us that if we, despite our flaws, can offer good gifts, then He is even more capable of doing so. By surrendering and trusting in God, we're essentially saying, "I may not understand your plans, but I believe you take delight in blessing me with wonderful gifts, so I place my trust in you." Sometimes, God's gifts may appear different from our expectations, as they often come wrapped in moments of uncertainty and challenges. Remember, Dear Sister, to hold on to the promise that He is a glorious gift-giver, and He will look after you.

1. *What is something beautiful the Lord has gifted you with?*
2. *Do you believe that gifts can be found on the backside/in the midst of uncertainty and struggles?*

Guided Prayer

Help me Lord, to let go and let you handle all the things I can't as you gift me with all the gifts that you know I need. Remind me at the start of each day that you find great joy in giving me the desires of my heart and the blessings of your will. Help me follow you first so that I might receive life abundant, not just for myself, but for my family and all whom I encounter. Have your way in each area of my life that you may bring about the perfect gifts for myself and those I love. Today Lord, I let go, because I know faith is built in the uncertainty and that good gifts are found on the other side.

Personal Prayers

_____
_____
_____
_____
_____
_____
_____
_____
_____
_____
_____
_____
_____
_____
_____
_____
_____
_____
_____
_____
_____
_____
_____
_____

_____ DATE

Day Seventeen

A JOY THAT WILL REMAIN

Scripture

"May the God of hope fill you with all joy and peace as you trust in him, so that you may overflow with hope by the power of the Holy Spirit."
Romans 15:13

"Weeping may stay for the night, but rejoicing comes in the morning."
Psalm 30:5

"But the fruit of the Spirit is love, joy, peace, forbearance, kindness, goodness, faithfulness, gentleness and self-control."
Galatians 5:22

Reflection

It is a deceptive tactic of the devil to encourage us to compare our lives with others. Such comparisons inevitably highlight what we lack or have yet to achieve. While Satan may present us with a half-empty cup, Jesus embodies the fullness of life. We are encouraged to embrace joy, pray without ceasing, and express gratitude in ALL situations because our hope lies beyond the outcomes of this world. Although pain, hurt, and disappointment will arise, dear sister, if you allow the Lord to nurture your spirit, you will experience JOY deep within your heart, a joy that will remain!

1. *What sneaks in and steals your joy from you?*
2. *Look at your life, what are you thankful for today?*

Guided Prayer

Lord, teach me to pray continually! I know that if I commune with you you will teach me your ways. I want to overflow with the fruit of joy no matter what I am going through. I want to give thanks in all circumstances. I trust you and I'm believing that you will fill me with unmeasurable joy. Help me to embrace each situation, good and bad, and find you in the midst. When I don't feel joyful, meet me in my weeping. Thank you for the promise that Joy comes in the morning.

Personal Prayers

_____

_____

_____

_____

_____

_____

_____

_____

_____

_____

_____

_____

_____

_____

_____

_____

_____

_____

_____

_____

_____

_____

_____

_____ DATE

Day Eighteen

STRENGTH IN HIS ARMS

Scripture

"I cling to you; your right hand upholds me."
Psalm 63:8

"Even there your hand will guide me, your right hand will hold me fast."
Psalm 139:10

"The eternal God is your refuge, and underneath are the everlasting arms.
He will drive out your enemies before you, saying, 'Destroy them!'"
Deuteronomy 33:27

Reflection

I often sugarcoat the realities of life when I speak with others, and
sometimes feel compelled to do the same when communicating with
God. However, it's perfectly acceptable to admit when we're struggling.
It's okay to tell a friend, "Today was tough," or to say to God, "This
situation is really hard." The Bible illustrates this repeatedly. The
psalmists cried out in grief, and prophets donned sackcloth and mourned.
Jesus wept. We all experience disappointment and carry feelings of defeat,
frustration, and despair at times. Yet, how beautiful is it that we have a
God who welcomes our honesty and vulnerability? Sometimes, He will
give us more than we can bear in our own strength, but our strength is
not found in ourselves. It is found in the strong arms of our savior. There
is freedom in falling into His arms, where we don't have to have all the
answers. In your defeat, you can take it to the cross, Sis...no sugar coating
required.

1. *Do you tend to sugarcoat things or think that your problems may be trivial to God?*
2. *Do you struggle with being honest and vulnerable before the Lord?*

Guided Prayer

Oh God, how thankful I am that you can shoulder all that I cannot. I'm so grateful that when I let you, you just hold me, without expectation. Help me bring my honest heart to you because I know that in your arms I will find strength. Lead me to Godly friends who I can trust with my truest self and let others feel comfortable in being vulnerable with me. remind me of your love when I need support and help me to be that support to others. Amen.

Personal Prayers

_____
_____
_____
_____
_____
_____
_____
_____
_____
_____
_____
_____
_____
_____
_____
_____
_____
_____
_____
_____
_____
_____
_____

_____ DATE

Day Nineteen

PARTNERS IN OUR PURPOSE

Scripture

"Two are better than one, because they have a good return for their labor: If either of them falls down, one can help the other up. But pity anyone who falls and has no one to help them up."
Ecclesiastes 4:9-10

"A friend loves at all times, and a brother is born for a time of adversity."
Proverbs 17:17

"Carry each other's burdens, and in this way you will fulfill the law of Christ."
Galatians 6:2

Reflection

Reflecting on the most challenging periods of my life, I recognize how God placed specific individuals along my path for specific seasons. There were moments when I was so focused on myself that I failed to appreciate their presence at the time. However, looking back, I am immensely grateful for the wisdom and comfort those friends provided. Relationships are important to the Lord, which is why He emphasizes that two are better than one and prioritizes love above all. We are blessed with partners in our purpose to help guide us. God will send you friends during tough times to support your endeavors. Cherish them, my sister, and return the favor when they need you most.

1. *Can you remember a time when a friend helped you through a difficult season?*
2. *Have you been a friend to another in their time of need?*

Guided Prayer

Thank you, God, for all the friends and family that have guided and supported me in the many seasons of life. I know you have placed them beside me to help me bear my burdens. I can recall so many sisters who were born for my times of adversity, and I thank you for that. Help me, Lord, to be a good friend and lift others up in their purpose. Teach me to lead in Love in all that I say and do, loving at all times.

Personal Prayers

_____
_____
_____
_____
_____
_____
_____
_____
_____
_____
_____
_____
_____
_____
_____
_____
_____
_____
_____
_____
_____
_____
_____
_____
_____

_____ DATE

Day Twenty

IT DOESN'T HAVE TO MAKE SENSE

Scripture

"On that very day Abraham took his son Ishmael and all those born in his household or bought with his money, every male in his household, and circumcised them, as God told him. Abraham was ninety-nine years old when he was circumcised, and his son Ishmael was thirteen; Abraham and his son Ishmael were both circumcised on that very day. And every male in Abraham's household, including those born in his household or bought from a foreigner, was circumcised with him."
Genesis 17: 23-27

Reflection

The Old Testament was written in a different era, making it challenging for us to grasp the significance of key concepts, particularly covenants. In today's society, giving someone your word often lacks meaning. My daddy used to say, "You can take my word to the bank," but that sentiment isn't the norm today. With 50% of marriages ending in divorce, many people failing to show up consistently for work, and promises often being disregarded, the weight of commitment has diminished. However, in Old Testament times, covenants held a different significance; they were binding, and each party demonstrated their commitment through actions. Abraham demonstrated his obedience by having himself and all the men in his household circumcised. He willingly sacrificed a part of his "manhood," without anesthesia, to follow his Lord, and he never questioned it. The tasks God asks of us may not always make sense, Sis, but it is our act of trusting that truly matters.

1. *Has God ever asked you to do something that didn't make sense in your earthly thinking?*
2. *Do you think you could have stood the test of old testament expectations?*

Guided Prayer

Lord Jesus, help me to be more like Abraham in my surrender. I'm sure it didn't make sense for him to have everyone in his household circumcised, but he trusted, and he followed through on his end of the bargain, even before he became the father of a great nation. Help me to trust that you will work in and through me as I trust in the promises of your word. Help me to let go of the logical and lean in on the spiritual. Help me to show you with my actions the condition of my heart.

Personal Prayers

_____

_____

_____

_____

_____

_____

_____

_____

_____

_____

_____

_____

_____

_____

_____

_____

_____

_____

_____

_____

_____

_____

_____

_____ DATE

Day Twenty-One

BEAUTY IS IN THE DETAILS

Scripture

"For we are God's handiwork, created in Christ Jesus to do good works, which God prepared in advance for us to do."
Ephesians 2:10

"In their hearts humans plan their course, but the Lord establishes their steps."
Proverbs 16:9

Reflection

Fun fact: I'm passionate about writing, but I don't spend much time reading. While I enjoy a good book now and then when my mind isn't overwhelmed, I'm not the type to simply sit down and read. I believe the main reason is that I'm not fond of excessive details. I prefer bullet points. Don't elaborate on how the grass sparkled with the first dew of a midsummer rain that smelled of lemongrass; just tell me there was dew on the ground. Yet, it's true that both in reading and in life, beauty resides in the details. We often get caught up in the big picture and crave the bullet points of life, overlooking how God is at work in the present moment. In the small gestures, in love and kindness, and in the everyday provisions, there is so much to appreciate. Take a moment and discover the beauty of His handiwork in your journey, Sis.

1. *Are you a bullet point girl or do you find joy in the details?*
2. *What beauty can you see in your current season?*

Guided Prayer

Lord, rather than stressing about what my night, evening and future will bring, I pray that you work in me today to breathe in your peace. Help me to take it day by day as I trust in you. Help me to accept the beauty in the details, even if I can't see the bullet points yet. Help me to follow your specific instructions just as Noah did when he built the ark because I know your provision will be shown in due time. Lord, help me to recognize that sometimes the details are pointing to a much bigger picture, one that has a greater impact than I can see. Establish my steps as you prepare me for the work you would have me do.

Personal Prayers

_____

_____

_____

_____

_____

_____

_____

_____

_____

_____

_____

_____

_____

_____

_____

_____

_____

_____

_____

_____

_____

_____

_____ DATE

Day Twenty-Two

EVERY DAY IS A RESTART

Scripture

"Because of the Lord's great love we are not consumed, for his compassions never fail. They are new every morning; great is your faithfulness."
Lamentations 3: 22-23

"He who was seated on the throne said, 'I am making everything new!' Then he said, 'Write this down, for these words are trustworthy and true.'"
Revelation 21:5

Reflection

Often, we are our own worst critics. The unrealistic expectations portrayed on social media can exacerbate our internal self-criticism. It can be challenging to embody the hands and feet of Jesus - being obedient, forgiving, and demonstrating the fruits of the Spirit. In my own life, whenever I am on the verge of achieving something significant for God's kingdom, I feel the devil's attack, robbing me of patience and self-control. I stumble in these areas, and then the enemy whispers in my ear, labeling me a failure. However, Satan overlooks the greatness of the God I serve - a God who is larger than our shortcomings, greater than our impatience, and capable of helping us regain control. God's mercy is renewed every single morning. Our yesterdays don't define us, because with Christ every day is a restart, Sis.

1. *Is Satan whispering to you lies that you have messed up so badly that you can't start over?*
2. *What areas are you struggling to surrender to God and receive his renewal in?*

Guided Prayer

Dear Lord, help me to let go of yesterday and live like I have been forgiven. I want to live for the glory of my redeemer today and forever. I do not want to let my yesterdays define my tomorrows. Lord, carry me through this day. Help me to forgive those who have hurt me and help me to be patient with all whom I encounter. Guard my lips to speak your love and not anger. Help me to be an image bearer and produce good fruit. Thank you that every day is a restart and that I can find renewal in you every morning. Lead me closer to you each day as I find my strength in you.

Personal Prayers

_____
_____
_____
_____
_____
_____
_____
_____
_____
_____
_____
_____
_____
_____
_____
_____
_____
_____
_____
_____
_____
_____
_____

_____ DATE

Day Twenty-Three

VALUED AND BEAUTIFUL

Scripture

"For you created my inmost being; you knit me together in my mother's womb. I praise you because I am fearfully and wonderfully made; your works are wonderful, I know that full well."
Psalm 139: 13-14

"Are not two sparrows sold for a penny? Yet not one of them will fall to the ground outside your Father's care. And even the very hairs of your head are all numbered. So don't be afraid; you are worth more than many sparrows."
Matthew 10:29-31

Reflection

For much of my life, I have valued the opinions of others over God's perspective. I have struggled with self-acceptance, disliking my body, hair, personality, and my skills as a housekeeper. For years, the devil has whispered lies to me about my unworthiness concerning both my appearance and abilities, and sadly, I have passed some of that misguided thinking onto my children. It was through their words that I began to see the absurdity of my own feelings of worthlessness. While it pains me to hear my daughters speak negatively about themselves, I can't help but wonder how it affects our Creator. God does not create trash; He creates treasure. Each of us is valuable, beautiful, and fearfully and wonderfully made by a God who makes no mistakes. You are special Sis, set apart for good works by a God who loves us so, so much.

1. *Do you struggle with negative self-talk or believing the lies that others say about you?*
2. *What things of value can you recognize in yourself today?*

Guided Prayer

Dear God, forgive me when I talk trash about myself
because I know that must grieve you. Thank you for
making me so intricate and for knowing me so well, inside
and out. Help me to find my worth in you rather than in
the opinions of others or myself. Help me to appreciate and
value others around me. Help me to use my wonderfully
unique attributes to glorify you and your name. Help me
to grow in love toward myself so that I can pour that love
out to others.

Personal Prayers

_____
_____
_____
_____
_____
_____
_____
_____
_____
_____
_____
_____
_____
_____
_____
_____
_____
_____
_____
_____
_____
_____
_____
_____
_____
_____

_____ DATE

Day Twenty-Four

LEAD WITH LOVE

Scripture

"But go and learn what this means: 'I desire mercy, not sacrifice.' For I have not come to call the righteous, but sinners."
Matthew 9:13

"Above all, love each other deeply, because love covers over a multitude of sins."
1 Peter 4:8

Reflection

Often, I find myself rationalizing my faith. I find myself thinking that if I do this, God will reward me, or if I don't, I'll face His punishment. Recently, while listening to a teaching on the expectations in the Old and New Testaments, Andy Stanley used an analogy about getting a new phone that helped me better understand. The old ways were fitting for their time and certainly divinely inspired, but with Jesus's arrival, a new perspective emerged. This new "version" emphasizes mercy as the standard. Jesus encouraged us to extend forgiveness, compassion, and love in all our interactions. Living according to His teachings brings life, but even when we stray from His path, He greets us with mercy and love. He also expects us to share that same mercy with those around us. We will never be perfect, but if we lead with love and mercy, Jesus will be glorified, Sis.

1. *Do you find yourself rationalizing your faith at times?*
2. *Are you struggling to meet anyone with mercy or love right now?*

Guided Prayer

God, help me to continuously replace my thinking with the ways of your son. Help me to offer mercy freely so that I may receive it freely from you. Help me to not feel like a failure when I make mistakes and take wrong turns, rather use them as a lesson to lead me back to your love. Help me to not judge my family and others around me, because I fall short every day in many ways. Lord, may my offering of mercy to others be my sacrifice to you as you desire. Thank you for your forgiveness and the grace you so freely send my way.

Personal Prayers

_____
_____
_____
_____
_____
_____
_____
_____
_____
_____
_____
_____
_____
_____
_____
_____
_____
_____
_____
_____
_____
_____
_____

_____ DATE

Day Twenty-Five

JESUS IS THE TRUE VINE

Scripture

"Finally, brothers and sisters, whatever is true, whatever is noble, whatever is right, whatever is pure, whatever is lovely, whatever is admirable—if anything is excellent or praiseworthy—think about such things."
Philippians 4:8

"I am the true vine, and My Father is the vinedresser."
John 15:1

Reflection

Throughout my Christian walk, I've encountered certain truths that I understood intellectually but struggled to embody in my daily life. Recently, through the guidance of wise, Godly friends, the Lord has shown me that my challenges with specific concepts stemmed from placing my trust in myself and my family rather than in Him. I believed that if my children thrived and I led them toward success, I would find fulfillment. However, when they faced setbacks, I experienced profound despair, and my sense of identity became muddled. People are inherently flawed, and despite their wonderful qualities, they will inevitably disappoint us to some extent. This is why it's essential not to base our trust, identity, and sense of fulfillment on others or on ideals. Jesus reminds us that He is the TRUE vine and encourages us to focus on what is genuine. The truth is, Sis, that the Lord is the only one who will never let us down or leave us feeling unfulfilled.

1. *Do you place your identity or your trust in something other than Christ alone?*
2. *Have you found your joy and identity contingent on some success or outcome rather than in the Lord?*

Guided Prayer

Jesus, continue to reveal to me areas that I am holding on to tighter than I am holding on to you. I believe that abundant life is found only in you, and I want to remain tethered to the true vine. Help me to dwell on you, the Way, the Truth, and the Life always. You are so lovely and praiseworthy and pure. Lead me in your ways so that I might become more like you every day.

Personal Prayers

_____

_____

_____

_____

_____

_____

_____

_____

_____

_____

_____

_____

_____

_____

_____

_____

_____

_____

_____

_____

_____

_____

_____

_____

_____ DATE

Day Twenty-Six

GOD DOESN'T GIVE BUSY WORK

Scripture

"Lead me, O Lord, in your righteousness...make straight your way before me"
Psalm 5:8

Reflection

I teach 11th graders, and teenagers aren't as difficult to understand as some might assume. They appreciate authenticity and prefer to grasp the bigger picture, as they dislike feeling like their time is wasted. Through my experience, I've noticed that they particularly detest busy work. Recently, during a quiet moment with the Lord, I felt Him gently remind me, "I don't give busy work either." Although we often struggle to see the larger purpose in life's challenges, God's word assures us that there's meaning behind every trial. We don't face these experiences without reason; each season and circumstance is specifically designed to strengthen our relationship with Christ. God wants us to know Him, produce good fruit, and uplift others. Stressful times can impart lessons in peace, while loneliness teaches us to find companionship in Jesus. Feelings of inadequacy foster dependency on Him, and inconveniences cultivate patience. Pain guides us toward forgiveness. Each misaligned priority helps us learn how to realign our lives in ways that honor Him. Rather than viewing trials as wasted time, Sis, we can find gratitude in each season that leads us to the cross.

1. *Is there anything in your life that felt like busy-work, but you are now able to look back and see the hand of God?*
2. *Are you seeking to lean into God more in the current trials of your life?*

Guided Prayer

God, I pray that you use my inconvenient seasons to deepen my dependency on you. When my heart cries, "Why me?" or my flesh longs to give up-remind me of your compassion and convict my angry spirit. Help me to feel your peace, even in the unjust and frightening situations I may face. Help me to forgive others and prioritize you in my heart and in my relationships. Lead me, Lord, and make your way straight before me that I might be found righteous in you.

Personal Prayers

_____

_____

_____

_____

_____

_____

_____

_____

_____

_____

_____

_____

_____

_____

_____

_____

_____

_____

_____

_____

_____

_____

_____

_____

_____ DATE

Day Twenty-Seven

SHIFT THE FOCUS FROM SUCCESS TO SURRENDER

Scripture

"Then Jesus said to his disciples, 'Whoever wants to be my disciple must deny themselves and take up their cross and follow me.'"
Matthew 16:24

"Commit to the Lord whatever you do, and he will establish your plans."
Proverbs 16:3

"Humble yourselves before the Lord, and he will lift you up."
James 4:10

Reflection

I heard a powerful statement on the radio some time ago, and it has echoed in my mind ever since: God prioritizes our surrender far more than our success. This truth is both profound and convicting. In everything we do, it's all about surrender. He holds our futures and simply asks for our surrender - not just a one-time commitment to Jesus, but a daily, all-encompassing surrender where He is Lord of everything. He takes our talents and uses them for His glory, guiding us through both the valleys and the mountains of life. He desires to lead us in our relationships, work, family, and finances. Although our efforts may not always be deemed successful by worldly standards, a heart surrendered to Christ will always lead to actions that make an impact in the kingdom of God, and that, Sis, is the truest form of success.

1. *How can you shift your focus from success to surrender today?*
2. *What areas are you hyperfocused on being successful and what might surrendering those to Christ look like?*

Guided Prayer

God, you know what my vision of success is as a wife, a mother, and in my career, but today I pray that you help me to change my inner narrative. Help me to see success through the eyes of your truth instead. Help me to have a heart of submission every single day. I know sin is doing things my way instead of yours and I don't want to keep sinning every day. Help my thoughts to look more like yours, help my eyes to see what you see, help the words I speak to echo your heart and help my actions to speak love always. Help me be successful in your kingdom work as I surrender.

Personal Prayers

_____

_____

_____

_____

_____

_____

_____

_____

_____

_____

_____

_____

_____

_____

_____

_____

_____

_____

_____

_____

_____

_____

_____

_____ DATE

Day Twenty-Eight

FAITH OVER FIGURING IT OUT ON YOUR OWN

Scripture

"So it was, when Abram came into Egypt, that the Egyptians saw the woman, that she was very beautiful." Genesis 12:14

"Some time later God tested Abraham. He said to him, 'Abraham!' 'Here I am,' he replied. Then God said, 'Take your son, your only son, whom you love—Isaac—and go to the region of Moriah. Sacrifice him there as a burnt offering on one of the mountains I will tell you about.'"
Genesis 22:1-2

Reflection

I find Abraham's journey of faith to be both refreshing and frightening. Regarded as the father of our faith, his belief was not without challenges; it was tested and proven. He didn't simply wake up one day ready to sacrifice his son; he learned from the struggles and failures of his faith that came before. In Egypt, he made the questionable choice to give his wife to another man, believing it was the safest and most logical decision. There were moments when he attempted to solve problems independently, as well as times when he watched his wife try to navigate situations on her own. We share this tendency with them; it's all too easy to rely on our own understanding. True faith, however, involves saying, "God, I have no idea how this will work out, and I feel anxious about what lies ahead, BUT I TRUST YOU." Sis, as our faith grows, we stop trying to figure it out on our own, and learn to rely on our Savior.

1. *Is there an area that you continue to try to figure out on your own rather than relying on God?*
2. *Can you ever imagine having the type of faith it takes to sacrifice your child?*

Guided Prayer

Thank you, God, for having it all figured out ahead of time so that I don't have to. Thank you that you hold me and my family in this broken, seemingly backward world. I have faith that you will help me handle each situation I am encountering in a way that you see fit. Help me to focus more on trusting and having faith in your truth than I do in figuring things out on my own. Help me to seek your will in the big and the small, today and all the days of my life as you lead me in the next steps of your kingdom work. Amen.

Personal Prayers

_____

_____

_____

_____

_____

_____

_____

_____

_____

_____

_____

_____

_____

_____

_____

_____

_____

_____

_____

_____

_____

_____

_____

_____ DATE

Day Twenty-Nine

HONEY IN THE ROCK

Scripture

"But I would feed you with the finest of wheat, and with honey from the rock I would satisfy you"
Psalm 81:16

"He made him ride on the high places of the earth, that he might eat the produce of the fields; and he made him suck honey out of the rock, and oil out of the flinty rock."
Deuteronomy 32:13

Reflection

I have been living this Christian life for over two decades. Throughout different seasons, I have pursued Jesus fervently, while at other times, I have felt lost, lonely, lazy, and lukewarm. Periods of death, disappointment, and depression have alternated with times of restoration and rest. Ecclesiastes reminds us, "For everything there is a season, a time for every activity under heaven." Recent experiences have shown me that His timing surpasses my own, that His provision is unparalleled, and that His love knows no bounds. When I read these scriptures, I am reminded of the truths from the Old Testament. God made a way when it seemed impossible, and His path became sweet even in the face of challenges. There is still honey in the rock and purpose in His plan, even when it doesn't seem that way, Sis.

1. *How would you define your current season?*
2. *What does Honey in the Rock mean to you?*

Guided Prayer

Lord, thank you for feeding me with the finest wheat and the greatest blessings in my life. Thank you also for leading me through the difficult seasons. I am so very grateful for the purpose in your plan and how that is playing out in my life. I praise you for your goodness, your love, and provision, and I pray that you continue to sustain me as only you can.

Personal Prayers

_____
_____
_____
_____
_____
_____
_____
_____
_____
_____
_____
_____
_____
_____
_____
_____
_____
_____
_____
_____
_____
_____
_____

_____ DATE

Day Thirty

THERE IS NO TIMELINE

Scripture

"Blessed is the one
who does not walk in step with the wicked
or stand in the way that sinners take
or sit in the company of mockers,
but whose delight is in the law of the Lord,
and who meditates on his law day and night.
That person is like a tree planted by streams of water,
which yields its fruit in season
and whose leaf does not wither—
whatever they do prospers."
Psalm 1:1-3

Reflection

In my teaching career, I work with diverse young adults, each on unique paths. Every individual faces challenges before reaching their goals. Reflecting on each student's path fills me with hope and serves as a reminder, both in Nursing School and in life, that there is no set timeline. It's perfectly fine if you feel you aren't "where you should be by now," as the timelines we often use to measure success are typically artificial and self-imposed. Christ does not evaluate our worth based on deadlines, degrees, or financial achievements. He guides us through our journeys with mercy and grace, no matter how unconventional or delayed they may seem. If you continue seeking Him, Sis, you will prosper.

1. *Is there a timeline in your life that isn't currently meeting your expectations?*
2. *Do you find hope in the fact that God doesn't work on timelines?*

Guided Prayer

Dear Lord, help me to remember that my timeline is not your timeline and that each journey, no matter how long or detoured it may feel, can be blessed and sanctified by you. Help me to seek you in each season and lay my timeline at your feet. Guide me each day and help me to put my trust in your plans before my own. I find delight in you dear God, help me to meditate on your your truth each day and walk nearer to you. May I find my purpose in producing your fruit rather than being prosperous in the eyes of the world. Amen

Personal Prayers

_____

_____

_____

_____

_____

_____

_____

_____

_____

_____

_____

_____

_____

_____

_____

_____

_____

_____

_____

_____

_____

_____

_____

_____ DATE

Day Thirty-One

ETERNAL SIGNIFICANCE

Scripture

"And the God of all grace, who called you to his eternal glory in Christ, after you have suffered a little while, will himself restore you and make you strong, firm and steadfast."
1 Peter 5:10

"You have made my days a mere handbreadth; the span of my years is as nothing before you. Everyone is but a breath, even those who seem secure."
Psalm 39:5

Reflection

At times, the thoughts that fill my heart are too vast to express in writing. I find it hard to comprehend why certain events occur, and I realize I may never have those answers. Karen Laing, in a message to a grieving mother, expressed, "More than ever, conversations with eternal significance are primary." Imagine how differently we might approach life and our daily feelings if we centered our focus on eternal significance. Our lives on Earth are just a fleeting moment in the grand scheme of things, yet the love and connections we nurture along the way carry profound eternal consequences. I believe that one day, we will catch a glimpse of how beautifully God has woven everything together. Until that day comes, Sis, we must trust that He is guiding us through this broken world and strive to leave an everlasting impact on the hearts of those we meet.

1. *What do you dwell on that has little to no eternal significance?*
2. *What tasks do you feel hold eternal significance?*

Guided Prayer

Dear God, I believe this is not our home, and I want to start living as such. So much that I focus on has ZERO eternal significance. Help me Lord to respond compassionately and bestow my God-given blessings on others, because I know those are the things that hold eternal significance. Help me to offer Godly instruction and daily affirmations to my children. Help me to be steadfast in your ways, build your kingdom, and leave an eternal mark on humanity.

Personal Prayers

_____
_____
_____
_____
_____
_____
_____
_____
_____
_____
_____
_____
_____
_____
_____
_____
_____
_____
_____
_____
_____
_____
_____
_____

_____ DATE

www.ingramcontent.com/pod-product-compliance
Lightning Source LLC
LaVergne TN
LVHW051417080426
835508LV00022B/3127